Tripping Daylight

Selected previous publications by Peter Dent

Settlement (Leafe Press, 2001)
Unrestricted Moment (Stride, 2002)
Adversaria (Stride, 2004)
Handmade Equations (Shearsman Books, 2005)
Overgrown Umbrellas (with Rupert Loydell) (Lost Property, 2008)
Ghost Prophecy (Kaleidikon, 2011)
Dasein and Scarecrow (Offline Press, 2011)
Price-Fixing (Kaleidikon, 2011)
With Number Plates Disguised (High Tide Editions, 2011)
Limit Situations (Smallminded Books, 2011)

Tripping Daylight

Peter Dent

Shearsman Books

First published in the United Kingdom in 2012 by
Shearsman Books
50 Westons Hill Drive
Emersons Green
Bristol
BS16 7DF

Shearsman Books Ltd Registered Office
30–31 St. James Place, Mangotsfield, Bristol BS16 9JB
(this address not for correspondence)

http://www.shearsman.com/

ISBN 978-1-84861-234-1

Copyright © Peter Dent, 2012.

The right of Peter Dent to be identified as the author
of this work has been asserted by him in accordance with the
Copyrights, Designs and Patents Act of 1988.
All rights reserved.

Acknowledgements
Thanks to the editors of the following magazines
in which these poems first appeared:
Fire (Jeremy Hilton), *HQ Poetry Magazine* (Kevin Bailey),
Litter (Alan Baker), *Poetry Salzburg Review* (Wolfgang Görtschacher),
Shearsman (Tony Frazer), *Stride* (Rupert Loydell),
Tears in the Fence (David Caddy).

Contents

Tripping Daylight   9

Arithmetic & Colour   51

Theatre   69

'The intensity of a brought-about recollection leaves one worn down; it consumes cells of the being if not the body. Truth goes on to eat through the weakened fabric.'

—Elizabeth Bowen, *A World of Love*

'Half of every experience is lack of experience.'

—Fanny Howe, *O'Clock*

1.
Tripping Daylight

1
It's not as though I'm taken in   by questioning who in his right mind would ...   it's answers that fail to ring a bell   aggrieved when listening to the hubbub that surrounds   I'll tend to lag behind 'off minor'   maybe excusing myself with a regular bag of tricks   take nothing but trust for granted   however you measure that time between the faded calendar and what lately passes for well-being   more mood than ever heads for a vacuum   if only the dodgy miracle would quit its act for make-believe   but more efficient   a certain frenzy's out and addressing itself to even the faintest accusation   a dream? or a silent movie   bodily   it shakes the screen

2
Not that this morning's light is too intense   I have a scheme that interests itself in 'desirable structure'   in evocations of a promising site illusion is proving less than useful   no security no substance I know of can help the sequence forward   the plot if it really is a plot excites more fear than hope   I'm presently unprepared to entertain such a climb   up scaffolding and ladders quick to a count of ten   rather I skip preliminaries?   and make the next stage work? best practice indicates it's only the higher connections matter   applaud the performance or approval can't be guaranteed!   cold forecasts weathering light   I shall scale the great unseen

3
She could do her own life inside two paragraphs
but only on a good day   a yellow brimstone
on a mounting-block would do just as well   if
you think about it?   last year was only a kind
of half-way house   as she knocked the ash off
another cigarette I knew it was simply a case of
character building   with the blocks supposedly
on order   somehow I had to reach the top and
not exaggerate the brogue   some prone to listen
out for 'conflict' rather than call for help   next
year I'll be handling facts with massive caution
not letting unwanted appointments hold me back
concealed entrances and a life unknown continue
to stake a claim   how sulkily she asks for more

4
With which he tried to avoid the outcome   out
of the frying pan and   not without noticing the
sense of incredulity which greeted his work   a
disadvantage to some he found it easy to borrow
someone else's temperament   death was having
a word just the other day   about blasphemy he
had companions enough to spare the blushes and
keep the peace   whose war has become a sullen
occupation after dark lets bloodshed draw long
queries from the fire   he stared and stared and
swore on all that was just he'd make connection
on which attractive note mists rose and caused
both entrances to disappear   the last of the day
and something from the sky with a face he knew

5
Fair trade   not merely when you count the cost
or swap contempt   home's never far she says
if keeping a tight ship knows the half   sunlight
as we know it taking just eight minutes to get to
the point   with lessons placed on hold it's dread
now figuring in every canvas but the last   in
which that need for contact takes a certain turn
I tell a lie she says and tells another   a portrait
fittingly dressed in red   tomorrow repaired she
feels like starting another   one with its burning
questions recollected   in places devoid of light
she's glorying in the change of heart as if there
isn't another threat!   whilst moments choose to
gather pace sail on   and never once make land

6
If this is what diplomacy means   or in a month
of Sundays seems to imply   forget whatever is
in a hurry to follow   I'm taking the chance of
a spell of weather to put my several policies in
order   and not for the first time vigilance is
due a spectacle to conjure with   distances of a
more ethereal kind are done away with   I'm
taking a gamble on ghosts till now untouchable
coming to play   my landscapes are abstract
enough   their faces all acrylic seem impressed
it's the way the senses take the obvious course
that inspires my appetite   I'm no longer playing
hard to get or styling truth   more death-in-life
is scarcely an option   when daylight's through

7
Some definition that some are privy to   and I'm
definitely not   it concerns me keeps my writing
awake at night   but I can't get past the first
instruction   now scratching the surface engaging
with maybe seven alternative deals?   I'd put no
finer point on it   we're as sound as truth   in
part believe me   it's better to re-enact the past
than to live it up for real   with life strung out
with history   when trusting masks can result in
telling it straight   last night was one too many
picking up pieces   read on for a comprehensive
quote   I excuse the daily oracle most things like
budget removals or rites of passage   rewarding
a perfect pitch can make the usual rate   per se

8
True   to the end of time and surely not before
against strang malladies my policies look well
assured?   quit reading those earlier paragraphs
or concentrate like fury   nothing's ever as it's
meant   to quibble over fiction?   it's a bridge
too fly for any syntax right in the mind to go
on   note the quantum leaps implied   lights off
then judgement   gift-wrapped for a much more
promising scene   joke joke!   it's entirely at my
own expense when out of pocket's not what it
was or will be   reminders are red like crazy
obscuring whatever's best   deception is better?
last legs then   down to horoscope or headline
judging what papers say   may we safely burn

9
Discreet occasions and pettie griefes I'll defend
to the last   she said no more and took a delight
in obfuscation   a blur of abstracts   making it
ofttimes quite a bit like old times   never more
willing   through parks and playgrounds of the
rich   where history projected its all-star cast in
heroic loss   could she make a mountain out of
less?   something preposterous there in the way
she'd censor art   when her own too garishly
exposed her sins   three graces turn up trumps
if terribly scarred by time   foreign again to the
eye but trembling easy to the hand   she takes
another lesson in sophistry to heart and pleads
for all she's worth   crime ordering a nasty fix

10
A perfect sentence that   and nothing in-between
I could see from one side of his work to another
light prevailing there   it's period black and white
and camouflage   but hadn't I seen it all before?
some delicate situation turning to sheer abuse for
kicks   his companions knew exactly how to read
his mood and take an exit   double-folded often
unspoken the predicted words were liable to make
an altogether other appearance   in days to come
his instinct was to cancel all those voices raised
by nature and disengage the self   why not why
not see quandaries off the graph?   a respectable
line you could say even one off-balance would do
the trick   and freefall …   parenthesis or bust

11
What I am returned to is the sense of balance in
an uninhabited sky   interior and unreachable the
equivalents   as last lights redden and thin   you
find that you're trapped between tall conifers and
a text   if never absent in a thought's unmaking
truly devout   and everything to do with keeping
an eye on futures   spies I volunteered to watch
through words find a half-light blinks on familiar
paths   yet more nights stripped of stars but they
just won't measure up   the perfect answer's out
there   breaking dreams   are we still unoccupied
by history   I imagine I'm back with you and it's
falling steadily as leaves?   the questions that we
sealed in a hollow tree   they're signed for good

12
Contrast like with like and you're getting close
since when has a forgotten statement left such a
stark reminder?   she looked if not suspicious
then sort of uneasy   shooting half-glance after
half-glance while visiting a tired authority with
familiar ease   to abandon story-time retune the
senses with 'what is' and dread a second guess
collective amnesia when she thought of it was
part of the contract   love in a foreign light or
getting lost required no practice   delicate as
the postcard's wintry scene all words escaping
to a clean horizon   a dulcet air and a breeding
ground for days   nothing remotely of substance
tried her song   unconsecrated and kept on ice

13
If ever a text looked odd it was this!   the very
last   such debate as followed never took kindly
to the risk   though being followed each day by
crime connoisseurs proved infinitely worse   not
that biography was involved   but whatever the
motive was there was 'precision fit'   or so they
said   each pilgrimage escalated now to a loss of
life   just eccentricity or the new élite?   I was
feeling nothing but rectitude and the rule of law
as if such stories mattered!   in dark by now
notorious churches clashes ensued   vivid enough
I'm sure for anyone's taste but more or less in
tune with the latest virtual theory   so withdraw
from intent   let justice gracefully tip the wink!

14
An introductory offer   or a timely intervention?
he'd queried and carried on packing his bags   a
bit grotesque but clearly to the point those acts
of madness had to go   never mind the tower
she'd ruined in advance   it wasn't just for now
but a world to come   to be aghast at thoughts
still ready to recreate the shimmer   of mystery
uppermost though in mind was candlelight   the
swirl of dresses   a dance to mistranslated fire
or perhaps a portrait dressed to kill?   the girl
made nothing of the facts   if he'd understood
intensity!   how soon he would leave her empty-
handed   Lammas and its gilded windows serving
all   like a homemade angel letting down its hair

15
Without a shadow   it's an unwarranted illusion
but never in all these years of mine more real
who'd verify the equinox anyway?   when I still
believe in heresy   a wavelength with the most
gorgeous smile it's targeted by oh I don't know
whom for scrutiny   maybe they'll let me in on
the scam   I just keep up the input attending to
business the only way I know   wide-eyed and
dutifully in and out of trance   but it's a shuffle
of clouds and rain reminds me   hanging around
is out of date   the bus tonight's impatient for
news not history with illumination a checkpoint
to crash through   everything for some's already
happened   initiation: can't come quick enough

16
Approaching a memory someone's left for dead
I feel too much   feel too far north of the place
it's happening   unnaturally cold and wanting to
come inside   don't think I can ever redraw the
circle   pour in words to suit   looking back on
the act it's still unanchored   a light exhausted
if calm enough to be with   your story it has to
be said not mine   I'm learning to pass on final
questions putting the future into reverse   love's
never in neutral?   well I've sometimes said so
not forgetting whoever's the ghost that writes
it up   now likely the last resort for some   try
those with a magic lantern   or a traveller with
a one-off gift for accident   commune with eyes

17
'Winter' was about to go to pieces in her mind
immanence on the other hand was getting itself
established   though one of the two was surely
a front for something out of sight   yes I am
it's true the camera!   I can't stand half-way
houses at the best of times   delete or save is
usually my motto   reinforcements not required
when the cold sets in   she's all for kicking her
way through frosted leaves the minute she sees
them   no place like it but I can't get over the
way she strings a project out   I'm swinging
back and forth like no tomorrow doing my best
for form   with 'compounds strange' it's better
the day accepts   some angles will catch a light

18
I want you to know how something and nothing
stands with the world as realised   in part   you
can make a weave of fact excluding philosophy or
trade ideas with the storms and multi-coloured
calms that afflict 'localities inside'   it's false and
frequently hand-to-hand   public pronouncements
as you hear them are liable to die of strangeness
still rhythm can override so I'm told   it's not a
problem   spareness in the word can bring most
crises into line   the beautiful often choosing to
terrify   for myself I happen to need a change
of accent   never the sound of bells   to debate
the merits of pleasure?   like the arias of nightin-
gales we're not to be put on hold . . . dream held

19
Broken in a flash   by shadowy flight it's a tale
of alignments in a single word   as yet there's
nothing spoken   will vision answer to the mind?
if quick to travel circles I'm useless monitoring
lines geared up to travel out   rock hard believe
me is the birthplace in the world I work   out
of a wish to guard   at least till the call comes
in my name is intrigue   not one of the crowd
though hints of a bright soliloquy flake away …
materially isn't it oh all the same   hard ground
and ivy   a complex acid scaling the wall   you
can make a case for devotion   acts that belong
to no-one are shaping up for good   all wings
a flutter   tucking light I should bury under life

20
Putting the glimmer back   where no-one's angel
cares to look   a soft spot under the greybeard's
hill or a bleak unread Collected   no matter what
it costs   you can bet the future's in *someone's*
reliable hands?   more sanguine and a couple of
decades older than the next I'm sure the counter-
culture's spoken for?   curated goodness   name
plates tarnishing the big white wall   I've seen
the camera tracking the way we came considering
several forgotten lies   but that's less fielding for
the par than nights out on the town   I've had
my fill as she regretted   prematurely good   and
bad at getting the corners coloured in   it's only
a matter of fact   candles burning both ends fast

21
Beautiful or nothing I believe   when you do not
know   it's taking any number of serious often
unsigned orders to reveal what's best   then pass
them off as yours   so it follows   a work more
idiosyncratic less simplistic lighting up the norm
as a book is under any old counter plain   I like
to see it!   just how sane the proof is in its nuts
and bolts approach   does it seem outlandish to
adjust the code   make over the 'I'?   no better
time for failure than when the past in its bid for
focus cuts excess   you're on your own absolving
quietness   taking a left-hand into town   who's
giving you a licence to print reminders   a ghost?
beatify anyone come midnight   when we're good

22
So you'd better be looking hard enough   there's
nothing but the range of seasons in a voice like
that   try a different tack   ease out of the solo
and breathe in unison   don't be surprised when
the sun goes down!   there's time enough for a
neat impromptu feeling   exchanges'll work out
fine   though if time offend then do the natural
his eye is on the logical deeps   it's true   don't
leave again   rather quit the playing at shadows
see the idea fit   and let the furies out to graze
on anything worth knowing   surely you'll bet on
azure taking a shine?   a given   if the blues as
pictured in his work are relative I'll count you in
it's phrases making him the most   strange light

23
Microprocess thought   and lo the bar is a model
of affectation   she can show them all her terms
a thing or two 'to determine best behaviour'   am
I competent?   to judge by what I'm saying skip
the handout   tomorrow she'll be asking manage-
ment to renege on the contract!   it's for me to
believe she's ready to tell and still on course for
gladness   remember possession?   more rooftops
lighting a fire with lasers   if I'm nearer the open
door well yes it's harder to take   face value is
looking the first thing up it finds   and suddenly
nothing's the same!   how she switches brilliance
to the right and leaves a text to fade   totality's
missing out again but do we really have to know?

24
It's a matter of daring   placing intentions ahead
of the text   part travelogue in part a degree of
automation you wouldn't want to see   I'm happy
to organise a coup some place   lifestyles handy
even the cash   though a good many others have
got there first   cack-handed probably and short
of a war   I'll be churning out all the pro-formas
an editor needs!   celebrity's best kept secret if
you're out for the count   numerically it's number
one that's offering a vision   years of adulterated
research   but now that we're past the solstice I
feel I can humanise the wheels   machine dictated
this is a set of anyone's favourite attitudes   kill
now or forever   I mean 'democratise' the crime?

25
You may never see it coming   and I'm not for
a minute prepared to talk it up   faint-hearted as
in the expression I'd never win the day   passed
over   in black and white   rectangular or barely
a line it operates like fiction   you can take it or
leave it   its casuistry's tantamount to law   my
word I'd rather quibble with the moon   tonight
there's a haze to give it admittedly ghostly colour
but I can sleep with that   I'm here like anything
to please that can find its way   to graduate in
life get access to the novel   if it's on its way at
least you're ready to pounce   someone some day
may be better placed but aficionados know what's
what   that any future has its history of disguise

26
Deadheading and other signs're down for quality
spending   check the sales for subtlety and good
new growth   enthusiasm really knows no bounds
next time you're back in town call in?   it's been
a while no question but maybe not to you   last
year in what maturity? I took too many calls for
comfort   believe me I'll have another Springtime
waiting in the wings and twilight put on hold   a
flourish and see the sky relents!   or how I view
it if the verse preserve   no so you don't believe
me?   but consideration demands access to better
illumination whenever the finches quit their seed
keep a check on costs best avoid the well known
dream   orchids test positive for love   by night

27
For a moment there I thought I was catching up!
just a glance and well investors were heading for
fiction with everyone on-side!   to read the last
known minutes was to make impossible music   I
seldom call up forests to manufacture shade but
misremembering comes easily   and the job was
quickly done   the marketplace pleased no known
audience with its song   the overwrought proved
quick to switch its stock   the way new fashion
writes the past   but again the weather's blustery
and the usual references are stressed   did I read
it right?   the line-breaks?   did they seem at all
confused?   too late I know but the price paid up
not one glade left me ready for the unsung dark

28
But only if you want   to register the vertigo of
place   a prevailing on the usual winds to lift us
silently   and leaving?   now it's coming to that
scarcely a tract to dwell on 'promises'   what's
irresistible and right to some   an atmosphere I'd
charted from the first   as you take more colours
than you need still making them work   deciding
to let the blue ice crack and crush to plenty only
the eves to hold them   is that ever enough?   a
disappearance of bliss and tangled limbs and even
as late as this *so* ghostly I can't believe the style
they're in   unsilhouetted lives   such distance
and fever generate a gift too rare to give   in
hours a collapse   unsteady heights   that freeze

29
Double figures   an area's now storm force and
the vessel helpless   it goes without saying   the
issue of the selling price's riding quote 'high' on
the agenda   'make poverty history' so a banner
calls   which is not as stated for the shy they're
retiring   waves over the top and no-one here's
to see the colours hear the sounds   translated
into shares   emergencies fast-slow   or is it up
to us?   to declare how prosperous the coming
year is   what's liable to clog the on-line artery
PCs themselves predict another quake but when?
it's worldwide   this accounted hurt   if a wave
strikes daily as today it does   will they make
their quotas?   agreeing to float a blue like loss

30
Barely a hint of colour   the holly is recreated
in flickering particles of light off rain or shine
now the sun's come through   I find I'm about
to remember something but I can't think what?
how finches visit come a fiercer cold   how the
seed runs out?   quicker than anyone can cope
with   like a conversation no-one's agreed on
'so where're we going?' plus theatre   I should
like but do I say ad nauseam   just keep your
eyes on the trees below my window   'quietist'
is only a possible word   for impossible times
'no different a hundred years from now'   said
softly   re. minor variations   there's a scene
not unlike my own   will you care to write it?

31
Psychics might've reminded me where she lives?
I travelled the optic route to no avail! a green
place near a crossroads where the dead hung out
proved useless   on every side but one there was
opposition to persuasion   and arguing the toss
couldn't make things real   did she dream me up?
I *do* forget and for reasons economic a M. Villon
alone knows   how the likes of us are strapped
and more than the law knows   how to deal with
looking for strangers oh it reads too strange for
words   my verses reserved for later should the
mob play up but isn't that *capital* conceit?   the
anonymous green places … they'd do the trick if
alphabet and minders cared   to spook the map

32
Bad light and a lot of spray   conditions exactly
right for going wrong   occlusion is the last
word in the index for repair but no-one cares
what elements of a day are checking expectation
borrowers go full tilt at the sales   never mind
stagnation   if I lost count years ago of views
that mattered well it kept me off the streets   I
now think wipers are up to something   after 5
the comfort zone's on edge   don't snap it up
unless you're sure   well pitched on an original
Saxon street (see our brochure) it's about as
modern as contemporary allows if you'll except
piazzas and the river—liable to lose the plot
when screens resist and the 3-D bid goes white

33
This has to be ours?   in weather that seems to acknowledge the fact   we turn a corner   to a gleam now more now less unsteady   like tinsel shaken   making with cloud near stationary overhead some welcome symmetry   but hardly new it's simply another year seeing if easy repetition works   events worth speaking about they have the edge on regular 'facts'?   so often how they will appear   with bleakness of vision counteracting turns of mind   it's not as though you're not at home   a roadside trickles with 'love' as you intend to think it   raddled blossom   like the present   how you stop to pick out colours never white!   blushing only for a season saved

34
Qualms and a red letter day   imagination asking for it and a backwash filling in   you can get a little too used to the story   coming out right is not to be dismissed however   there's a chance he can get one generation out of a fix   already there's a hint with some crackling energy around did you hear it   ever?   the subtle if stormy air that's sounded   shrill on purpose after dark as would focus *any* reputation on a soul   I've only his word he's getting over it   excess in passion? it's the gift of some who're dreaming beauty out of bed   good heaven's got to be there possibly on spec   or the magic's crashed   he's putting nothing in order?   still his house sleeps through

35

Freezing according to the page?　perhaps　near
mauve to the NNE and there is a forest to come
familiar outlines　where several periods of her
life were spent　today like yesterday unfixed I'll
have it marry 'innocence'　with a string of less
desirable words　so entertain a life　she alters
just the unfamiliar　to suit or rather exacerbate
what's new　I meant to bring her flowers she'd
recognise?　more distance a day of grace better
clung to　tripping daylight like a switch　have
done or no?　if it seems to reposition love well
leave alone　as days like clockwork run to seed
the image of hers I can't make mine is wearing
yet another shade of green　intense and untried

36

Did he go to the attic often　am I meant to say?
his last word as I have it is surely the perfect
introduction　'tomorrow's done' with boxes like
no-one's business all unsealed　did he mean to
pry I wondered　though he never meant to hide
there was seldom a page where all was said　less
signed　a still air　a musty invitation to settle
not one but bundles of small improbable accounts
no truck with continuity no attempt knowingly to
fly a kite　he'd kept his word and speculation to
a minimum　imagining it　'something out there'
that grew　too brilliantly uneven ever to prove
a point: a measure more than this bulb can enjoy
will I always wonder　did he ever come down?

37
7 a.m. clear skies and I'm throwing out scraps
not the least geometry   by half   or not at all
with a head like thunder   there's a line that's
coping seriously well and so much so it's comic
the dream *itself* resembled thunder!   way back
when the water tower ticked all day or seemed
to   you'll forget the principle when interest's
out ahead   I forgot to ask how but they never
so much as dropped a hint   fine floods indeed
is there anything worse   who's coping anyone?
strict measure fits a bill—honestly I do forget
if I remembered why!   it was horses and carts
in those days things moved twice as fast   you
cared I know   so is this the reason why do I

38
And displayed the minimum of 'elevation' did it?
I can't say this one did but yes it was definitely
challenging   the finest ones have a gift you'd
dream of (if only it were life)   life has the edge
in several other respects   I think I prefer those
middle sections when you're getting to know the
ropes   short stories   who'd believe them ever!
seeing it so   I'd really like to offer my thanks
for the last   a lazy Summer's day kept endings
quiet   and though I'm saying so quite crisp . . .
enough   as soon it really will be   I'll send you
the gist   how hard the plot's been subsequently
or do I mean back then effected   nights nicely
in order   look everything you wanted   shining

39
'Combined brilliance and brutality'   it's best to be on the lookout … telescopically kings don't compare but the worst is always to come   if it seems that symbols merely aggravate you can treat with care   meaning?   oh slip some other ingredient into the mix   hardly ever and a day goes by without something   it's our pure white nature trailing blood   less life more violent but did it count?   if you dream the ordinate you're bound to finish on top   at least one window of the book looks happily on   history it's a lady's smile and worth a mention   'quick change'   to welcoming the visitor   showing the office at its best   free entry?   subscription carries a price

40
And being   somehow immaterially dispossessed it's not easy   life by its very trick takes a bit of doing   the business whatever   oh it's easy enough   you can find it in the directory   any subsequent move worth making is a move uphill consider its minor prospect   dictate your news there's a ready audience to hand!   on site hard hats are essential plus a gift for deconstruction fly away Peter then but only if you're going the distance   things seldom weighed so little   as I remember   and can't it being this late object surely the heart's not extra-mural?   when you con the where and by what proportion it's time to come off-stage   read me a riot   Acts I–V

41
A minor revelation or two   now back from the
real beyond I can see it   not altogether clearly
but with a brave and perhaps more practised eye
natural as only the world is   proof's too quick
to accept   harder today as it goes ice whispers
something in passing   off overland and home to
the current kill   a force to reckon with singing
down nerves ... I'm adrift in visions of the why
and wherefore?   better to keep the immoderate
word at bay   am I never again to practise fast
and loose with light   good money it's safe with
me and the frozen past   life has it all in mind:
the pitfalls often scintillating works-in-progress
don't look if you like   see everything you want

42
How best to do it?   problematise the very act?
another way to see what's going on is to spread
a rumour (minus several crucial details) to the
opposite effect   which is crude of course but a
lovely wildfire   watch the faces!   but still take
readings with the proverbial   you never know if
two can play   today the elements are ready for
sequence   my true persona's been appeased and
happy to interconnect   still I'm taking chances
here   in any hot-house exploration you'll find it
easy to separate what flowers from the ooze of
healthy decay   scout around for signals   even
unspoken promises have their trademark smile!
the provenance of the next best thing's unknown

43

In this final exercise you must acknowledge the
part emotions play in setting—naturally this is
just the first scene—all things up   in taking
your cue be prepared to represent domestic and
social clues as random energy   not easy to put
in quotes let alone answer for itself   again all
balances are due the utmost   non-commercial
use one might think easier if more adventurous
but words passing between us and the rest are
bound to disturb   the camera's not an eye but
suddenly *there*   the angle ± the flash   a piece
of paper shimmers and incredible objects stare
into any tale you propose you can always fit a
mood   laugh or cry we're give or take a ghost

44

Looking for echoes in a crazy decade   it might
well have been her forte   but for noises off?
camaraderie under political fire and those piece-
meal mild addictions   would she have stayed
the pace or worse still written the sequel?   my
doubts I do forgive   when you've witnessed a
favourite trapped off-side it's time to quit   in
street-speak such is the glamour for the crime
you get away with!   dismiss it at your peril
that's how a voter votes   content's not found
by counting clouds   she's keen on treating guilt
and the field with exaggerated colour   to many
of the cases this was it: *the place*   more plans
than futures here reduced to bouncing off walls

45

'Pulled threads in pink and mauve'   so now it's
talking and getting things off the ground   long
gone I'd thought with the thinking through   his
latest work?   a dissolution some believe   long
driven   his sky too candid   proud of the style
and keen association   when accepting anyone's
side of the bargain I'd personally begin by trying
a series of casual half-movements   promising
hell or more to pay   but as you will   he was
happy enough alone with a range of self-awarded
views   harder by far to call 'my own'   though
heavens I tried with not incurious answers gists
of which dissolved spontaneously like cloud   if
anything was worth it this was?   dearest desire

46

Or wasn't there joy at the very thought of being
tempted?   maybe not till now she thought   as
much as the sudden movement ended in disarray
imperfect balance though   it had its own reward
when held in check   she'd see the impossible as
just more writing on the wall   and goodies like
pears and apricots toppling over   reminding me
how only last year the inappropriate and half a
bottle had become the norm!   now it's a fatal
likeness with a matching prayer   your servants
N and N …   make these and all things in one's
strange capacity distant   at any rate somewhere
out beyond the point of no return   to each and
everyone a stranger affair   thus easier to love

47
And what might anyone give for a quandary like
that   good for nothing and better than average
as time is so the worlds participate and die   or
faced with the challenge disengage   become the
kind of ghost contemporaries might stare at . . .
a river 'tying itself into knots of vagary'   it's
proper surely to view each landmark as ambition
somehow a single idea regardless of taste   I'd
rather integrate the puzzle and watch the minutes
go   passivity or the seething of an unconscious
mind?   the eventful doesn't does it depend on
words?   the ordinary's in spate   here's shadow
'unto midnight' … what a sentence is to death
life's full   the river's branching   no two ways

48
Humble … which is not a word you hear much
save if you will the groves of yesterday   anew
… and forgive the single man his odd unsound
direction   the site is more aloof than the house
you've never lived in   outside parameters and
effortlessly making law   did I want to know did
anyone try the Silent Pool   or meet its mists?
environs that once proved fit for kings now find
subjects steering clear of paint   'my field is a
practical contribution to the state'   observing it
from afar   executives can wave their notes like
beasts in torment but no blood spills   the only
figures in question tolerate pure wisdom … like
light that travels unquestioned through the head

49
A promising day for the selling of pardons   or
so he thought with martyrdom never an option
it's a bad day he's forbidden to preach   relaying
government initiatives to the poor on trust   'I
pledge to introduce good living free of abuse at
the point of light'   never mind babblers and
their equally heretical like   wouldn't there be a
new power in the nation hitting targets?   I mean
a windfall energy topping the coffers whenever
a monk showed up   was he responsible   did
he emphasise the past?   too loyal for some he
harried the awesome   picturing scripture as his
mid-term bonus   not just a share of angels but
a good-time minimalist scheme   confessing art

50
Representative in court he holds a glad debate on
earth: ace-high corruption?   false relics of the
restless book!   he makes full use of robe and fee
regretting how 'insufficient' the public funds are
loved by some   with ever increasing pressure on
the purse   still under influence banked in juris-
prudence   to quote the craft unquotes a people
and manoeuvres all in the name of risk!   but no
he loves consensus   he'll leave us a 'better man'
electing futures or economic caution to the chair
should it look that good 'electric'   so we're still
a worthy charity?   a private number to be called
to greatness   catch him working up the gong he
loves to the sound of music   swelling out a gain

51
Sophistication it's not my style she said   a gift
to some   what else   the usual shenanigans but
then as sweet as they come and irrepressible   I
could put my clock right knowing those squalls!
to such unruly ends revive the norm ... with its
scatterings of roses and heaven knows what   if
the gale stops gusting she'll scrutinise the word
for progress or take the appropriate action   to
guess our rise and fall   the first one home's as
good as done   should it come to it her word is
'distinction'   grafting value on to chance is that
bizarre?   it was never a problem   blush pink
or original white revive like you'd never believe
not a contra-indication but a god-struck answer

52
True enough the unexpected palls   a grey cloud's
in and it's static   'a compass is a charm to keep
what's worse away'   but convince the neighbours
saying my plan's a mess   that it leaves us at the
brink   I know   of an evening so still it remains
whatever else a puzzle?   how right to consider:
the shock wave and who wants to start   can you
guess?   when it reaches you first you're the last
to know   explain what destinations are up to at
the time   you can see more evil clouds than this
but find no better colour for dispersal   even the
'yew trees' aka imagination make more darkness
hugging corners of the mind   tell me why aren't
the blackbirds singing?   I'll not remember when

53
'Grubby yellow' sounds about right for a canvas
ready to emphasise the present inadequate light
I'm feeling curious about entering the place what
with its overwrought but immaculate imitations
and something on the verge of maybe happening
I'm only too aware the two of us are coming to
grips uneasily with atmosphere   that meditation
where a cube of shadows lets in colour   and
uneasy windows peer out constantly to manage
the world   it's hardly a reconstructed drama or
a 60s happening   pale cornfields slow to notice
the full moon overhead or the sun that's about
to set   there's retrospective written over every
scene   a painted question for the harvest home

54
It is likely you'll want to know the whereabouts
and some of the vital turns   a number of new
procedures seem to have relocated   to unknown
states   not a single train goes by   but details
are getting sketchy …   art as you're getting it
here is loaded   dictums work by living it up or
letting solutions too alarmingly red for comfort
clear   in itself near-death experience is not a
problem   I don't invoke the past I'm not under
contract to a rule   certainly there's nothing to
hide away   unfinished business looks quite the
part though the journey's out of time   so many
poplars down the line   all straight and proved
that you wonder often   can any of this be true

55

No it's ordinary enough when you think about it
and when you do it's pretty magical   not nearly
a secret   'still you can't help keeping it quiet'
so she said   and pointing nothing more obvious
out than 'understanding is not the issue' she left
unharassed and fast   thought still material   to
declare   in steel and glass with colour lifting it
almost head-high off the ground   disquiet at
one or another of its dialogues put on hold   for
many of us   'experience' is a returning to the
misty-eyed to the muffled response   however I
can't identify with everything   low lights make
for a place I've never been nor want to   times
familiar   all that I lean to is lining up the cold

56

Intermittent they may be many of them working
on transmutation   but likelihoods shouldn't stop
anyone doing a deal   lights up for a season?
almost any number you can think of trying out
bulbs   look if it seems too luminous like green
flares over marshes then choose another world
the old place keeps its shadows handy   and true
to form as a rule   its signs are clear enough no
matter what they're staying the distance   that's
understood   likewise the present for all its one-
time virtues it's compensated for   collapse is
sudden and hardly ever healed   I fear too much
a change in values   how energy companies up a
volt   witnessing how it is   the light burns low

57

Cymbal ...   from plain to highly orchestrated in a series of asides   urban and maritime   we're electronic as any   a city keen to examine itself now heavily re-sampled   long processed with a heart I'll die for   concord!   sonic as a script! life spirals when its many voices wittingly catch the synaesthetic eye   looping like my track is currently here enhanced   by how much it can't be quickly determined   pavement walking's easy slipping into a different more appropriate code I love it most whenever the jagged and melodic intersect or overlap   speaking as often they are their mind   the odd bus turns again in the old parts   trafficking a chancy score   ... *Cymbal*

58

Wrong of me then   to propose another façade? I've handled every contribution   original or not with interest   I ask you make what you want of the past   no longer up-and-coming it creates a quite forgettable day   names wounded by a flop or tempted by such-and-such a bank a division of something seriously other   glass fronted to afford ability   oh I've still lifes in arrears   you know   robustness is not a guarantee   I'd rather subsidise a bulb ...   renewal reversal how much how drab but I thank you unlucky stars in your stark advance   cash shines no shine and nowhere it's not my style   I handle purchases with proof of care   take umbrage courteously to the door

59
Between cliff top and the rail insects tinier than
a midge describe could it be to me a universe?
imprecision   simply I'm thinking this up unaided
by the book?   no all I'm getting now is static
closed doors on the world   and possibly others
a constellated fire   with oh delectable leftovers
natural I think   getting it wrong in astronomical
numbers   caught as today is under a cloud not
yet a synonym for quietist nor a superpersuasive
dream but time to remind you I'm jotting down
endless theories given a chance!   my truth's not
so curiously undeniable believe me   its seaview's
casting everything in minor lights   walk on and
check for yourself as others skip the ghostly do

60
Which was where I'd found myself   somewhere
tricky between the vision and the fact   really I
shouldn't but I'm counting on you   the music's
louder freer   if now not always though I liked
the way opportunity turned out   since missing
the introduction mapping a totally different moon
affairs one after the other exploded in a pall of
light!   fabulous reason it was that kept me safe
from the law but did any one of me care   I div-
ided more than my time avoiding adventure (my
reach if not geographic was in due proportion to
the gift of loss!)   question the canon and you'll
miss a trick   biographies of 'a world' surrender
what   indefinite articles transparent as the child

61
Speaking of lamenesse there's much at least one
corner of the mind to do   and I'm doing it not
in the original but the revised   which shows up
perfectly   come what accidents may   minder
and philosopher both a help in troubled times or
phantom busybodies?   it's perfectly reasonable
accounting for loss by quoting a 'world outside'
some change in solar circumstances or radiation
from beyond   it's never the same excuse as I
say it often   how the clearer branches dip and
sway to a breath of wind shinier than most but
joy's impatient   keen on easier options   as the
words strong-arm the skyline ... still invisible?
following the bluest sail I know about my mind

62
So this *now* is the annexe   a score still to settle
and invitations to prepare   loved mornings will
underline what's said or not with just the hint of
a smile   those forgotten things innocent of what
in the name of fact they meant!   the racket of a
day in advancing light ungoverned and desperate
to break new hours   I'm thinking as much of a
playpen as the law   to be told repeatedly don't
fritter away another 'history' ... it's music to no-
one's ears   perhaps we're playing consequences?
in '01 there was nothing more to it than staring
up what else would you see   impressions linger
just as they're meant to   with clip-on lights not
to mention doubts high and invisible on the roof

63

Heraclitus will put it one way   and she another
you've got it: opposites in one   while whatever
the residual heat it's never a river   as I forget
only too often   alternative invitations: consider
the whys and whatfors?   when camping up has
a style of its own there's competition in chance
a minute only   that's all it takes and she still
can't draw the line?   I can feel it though!   it's
like something burning the landscape   one you
love enough to win the love scene back redrawn
and shaded   though only when she fancies it—
the watery dip itself   it was twice attempted as
I remember we're better off with standard matt
unframed like light with meaning up to the edge

64

Dust clouds at the brink of unrest   shadow on
cloud   it's inevitable the convoy and predictions
are given away   when he elevates the tension or
calls up trust history in its rarest form begins to
play   so independent the correspondent that his
notes no matter the frequency come alive   if the
cap's on its lens then distances aren't too remote
for infantries to come into play   children know
the program exactly   for what it is   a flash in
the eyes   accepting all-out bombardment like a
yawn of fate   it's 2200 now by all means put it
on if you want the latest ... the place our next
star's born?   we're overcompensated   lightning
over a countryside rolled up   the military abed

65
Is this the chosen moment to begin   getting or
taking a rise   the weather's definitely closing in
anyway meditation doesn't mind the dark   it's
worth a good while travelling incognito   streets
of a promising likeness   unobserved as ever but
they're saying there's no way out of town   do
you buy that?   don't you ever dream yourself
into quintessential debt?   a maker can make the
existential difference   letting pictures moon-size
threaten to speak   I swear it takes the pressure
off   face value now you're joining the queue as
priorities suggest and who says no when every-
one's throwing caution to the dogs   bumper to
bumper our minds go quietly   tipping us down

66
Shadow lives why not?   leave the score unread
a poor fool's happy to undermine a text already
coming apart   twin frets and a lower case   a
lyrical hardly natural bent?   it's the credulous
recreate the book of the brave   think of a life
found pale and decreated   metropolitan longing
in it for the ride   too cute?   I think it often
how some minor blues can make the difference
slow drag slipping away to clear the beat   and
back   it's strange he exults at this   the pull
of gravity   the next I know there's something
tearing at (and who'd believe it's taken two) the
heart   much more I think to measure   swears
a good thing in   as I feel the form   fails safe

67
Flushed with the thought of conquest he'd made
his way skilfully out of trouble   it had been a
curious affair and writing it down made clear to
everyone his quarrel with style   resources put
him every discursive time to the test   by no
means gifted with words he saw his chance now
to engage in personal protest   by turns remote
and closer than his heart she found him difficult
to read   more breathing space than energy with
affection underwriting every turn   indelible if
passing she couldn't say but grew in wonder as
ambition grew   whose custom it was to double-
cross any life too invisible to mend   set limits
lovers might reach and triumph over   the best

68
These plain wooden slats   this too early Spring
can translate dazzle into an almost contradictory
world   do I think I recognise the lyric design?
as soon as look at it it fades if briefly   crocus
the whites and mauves a pool of violets under a
wall   light flashes randomly on what a sentence
is a Logos fills   as waters change and flow   if
you want then repeat it   often when the on-off
lines are lifted by a moment's breeze you get a
feeling everything and nothing whatever the time
or sunlight is   it's still a first time   looking us
hard and original in the eye   via folding hills
and underworlds alike   place just another room
at the pull of a cord   here turns me on and off

69
Think hard and deliciously   if not I'd rather you count the shifts and contradictions of a day   a job lot set to 'steady state' just the one position luminous green   if you will just watch the dial and see me in   it's immediacy showing its face let's get the two of us off the hook and make a night of it   but I clean forget   so much of the mind's engaged in pulling in driftwood!   tides outstrip demand   anyway anyone can read their progress when coincidence kicks in   the pair of us meeting here?   I'll leave the last but one to you   dreams plain enough ... if you don't make course corrections   I'm advertised in blue   a slender blue line   love making my own way out

70
It's normally a private demonstration   rejecting maps?   if you're looking for a plot the chances are it's on indefinite leave   not that I'm a kill-joy but this side of the watershed there's just a limited number of reservations   take two or try to separate life from glory   withering smiles as rendered speak of compromise at best   such is urbanity as practised in the raw!   try to avoid simplicity   it's unlikely you'll meet more classy resistance this part of town   foreign opinions only button a lip   the collection you're looking for comes with dazzling insecurity and a tincture of the past—the individual and his aberrations considered or thinly realised   appointment only

71
All he could see from the top of that mountain?
yours truly impressive heights   some said (and
couldn't not today) for the taking   pleasurably
enough already a clarity in hand   beyond which
heat haze or dry skyline or the foot of the page
so in the evening of the hour to bed   affection
swelling like poison in the blood or sweetness in
his side   I'll rest he said and with that in mind
prepared the world   for what he'd decided love
might say tomorrow   and tomorrow?   what an
entirely other place a closer walk beheld   indeed
what distance now was   flowers springing up to
something you can't help thinking   everything's
conditional and in such a state of mind   take all

72
Which is about as complex as it gets   a faithful
replica to fall back on on a bad day   don't you
know I'm happy to comply?   at least go through
the motions putting a good word in   like AD79
the coastline's altered as the flow extends   how
and why may and not obviously depend   later I
hear they sank a well   encountered mosaics also
a carbonised but readable text thank MSI   now
closer to a meaning I'm asking if dissolution's in
its abruptness equally in its element   and where
this leaves romance and precision drawing today?
later and no exaggeration I learned I suppose we
all do to just get on with it   think about what
a master-stroke is and what is the matter of fire

73

She happens to prefer the original?   the default
setting's equal to anything yesterdays can throw
at it   'I'll have that desert for my own!'   she
says   she'll make it through the meanest of her
failed equations to a place where signs are equal
dreaming it up   will anyone entertain her first
let alone second idea   such matter conforms to
expectation   eyes concentrating every colour on
aspects of the past   'I'm seeing if I really want
to think that thought'   its intolerable one-time
destination that isn't   change keeps at it trying
to talk its way through red   well met but never
as dust is making something of itself   identity's
a killer   she takes herself back   innocent to be

74

A labyrinth of elegy and invocation   it could be
the best part of the day with its face to the sun
in February?   anything might happen   and I'm
(it's expected) reliant on you   for interpretation
skies newly motivated   with no sense at all of
unease when bulletins go up   I watch them so
closely for a fatal flaw but hard as I look there's
little else   the dead keep falling grateful as per
the words but I doubt the expense   if I take a
look I never tell … yet the last cloud crossing
the sky took something like forever   that's how
sensitive things were when I asked for more of
the oh so beautiful same   narratives seeming
to evade a climax   read on   day clears a way

75
'Without which it might never have happened!
playgrounds of a ne'er-do-well   you can bank
on his output?   but the voices cut in two by
two   for the best of reasons the story's less
like instruction and more like a full-bodied red
relaxed occasions under the classic vine   here
Virgil and others more impetuous were inclined
to call up vision   practice in the surreal was
not an option while the sun glanced generously
on Amminean fruit   Book II is full of it but
skip the flourish   I can't help feeling *presence*
is the way of *every* world while passion's just
to simplify the lot   suspend the maze belief's
in a bottle   provenance lacking a label sucks'

76
Two squares of dark and superfine?   it took an
imaginative calculation walking it off and all too
often the streets were crazed with broken lamps
the 50s went by quicker than most   thinking it
over   the rush to renew or (inconceivable now)
to repair   things one by one had a multilayered
aspect   you could count them up and how such
adventures mattered in the telling   girls stood
on swings and a bike for example filled as many
rough books as its talk   willow and stream I
knew articles of peculiar intent   on night alerts
I was plotting monologues not for gain but for
misadventure   what else if I tell you   stars lie
closer   a blaze of angles   lyrics taste the same

77
No songs   and nothing striking on the hillside
the tower won't have me stopping to talk   by
trying everything once (if that's the considered
option) I can eliminate much of the waste   I'll
put it down in longhand first then look out the
inhibitions!   where one owl flies woods make a
choice referral   it's too late for crying but an
echo's located   somewhere up there in a room
with a view   don't ever underestimate it magic
always picks the least accessible hour!   when a
story thinks me up I'm only too happy to wing
it   fast on a prayer   if I'm nudging you else-
where please forgive my practice   make me a
tempting offer   a home I can find in the dark

78
Exploratory   only willing to view beyond?   like
minded share a place on the fence   getting their
wisdom by proxy   obscure as it seems   I'm all
for diplomacy where signs are concerned—the
risks are never entirely obvious or the ad's not
up to it   the artist's 'colours' are spectrally out
but only by a fraction   subjects glow *in code*
with energy planned for slow release   however
when the word is more 'about' than 'is' matters
take a different turn   I'm first to admit there's
something different on the line   if you listen in
you can gauge the intervals the changes of pitch
make appropriate deductions from the blurb   a
fact too 'visible' to light has still life turn a head

79
Well her recommended 'meander' keeps me up to
scratch certainly   preface past second dedication
up to Chapter One 'The Whole of the Night'   no
footsteps in the street and a medium frost ready
to conform   thinking it was the last thing I had
in mind   to be obsessive … I made a stab   a
multiple entry but no-one saw it no-one suffered
in the making   histrionics ever a bargain but the
small hours missed my point   you'll die as soon
as know it—the first draft's titleless the second
refuses to bite and a third woos violence hard …
has it twisting and turning fiction to distances of
a morbid self   my dark course's running true?
all the published nightmares now cut to the quick

80
The word *would* had a special resonance for him
and not entirely for sentimental reasons   when
it came to the last night of his old career there
were more bargains to be had than mirrors . . .
think of classification and much like a screen a
mind goes blank   perhaps it's an ideal context
setting words in glass exactly   any aberration
given the angle will gleam   astrological 'veritas'
nothing so steady is there as a gift for heights?
but he's seen it all   knows knowledge as well
as graffiti staring in the underpass and sidings
of a world   it's aggravation leads astray   why
now why never   love excites a familiar eye to
death!   'to another day'   he would offer more

2.

Arithmetic & Colour

1
Abstraction is keeping a natural born ghost up painting by numbers   it's simply how it is and you can see it   Monday is never averse to life or when the feeling takes me packing it in   as shadows near too often to collapse   and all it stands for even   do I look as if I've been here brush in hand 'non-referential' from the first?

2
See any good architect making his way to work that edge to edge delight and often sundry   no he'll not forget this Winter   too secret in my distance watching cormorants remove   he *will* succumb or will he to matter stretching out his line   he thinks how a garden safely builds with crystal   wings leave a mental note on sky

3
Each painting tells an extended story a specific dreaming especially when told in the open   he tells me thermometers are showing several new degrees of frost   a look whether I want it or not on the fastnesses of time   impermeable as a word at the height incredibly of Summer still fresh to survey   impasto or snow free speech

4
It's not easy getting from here to the lighthouse
the caves don't measure up to expectation ever
in Winter or such as passes am I ever in doubt?
read how!   it's only natural you'd leave a little
on the pale side   weather recalls it   the sector
where coasters disappear   it's all he said about
'doorways' and seeing the hand before your face

5
She's still not up to thinking   I'd chance a sea
change any day updating listings till a last name
glows   and whatever its merits cut to the sky-
line   sapphire and fragile as any the data can
signal   a channel to ply   then home or haven
and the cost?   not a light to mention   just as
we found it the absolute interprets like a dream

6
Trees excused since yesterday so it seems   I'll
set the likely moment   green's breath is natural
in its element   blue is painterly not yet adding
up?   true enough   my history writes itself and
everyone knows what that means   numbers can
function only *too* well exceeding a day's demand
so colour me in please   don't ever rig the boat

7
Just as you left it   the picture wants us moved
prosaic never-nevers to a land (it would be *that*
colour) of dream shades falling over a good eye
not one seen too easily at its best   if only you
knew!   just how much the foreground's changed
it takes translation right back to source   as an
ice-breaker quits the mirror and perhaps the fact

8
The conclusion might well be a sideslip   to no-
where   let's start repeatedly in-between where
the sun's acclaimed   mid-stream it's rather a
formal invitation   a glitter to think about eyes
and whoever in the face of it could journey on
such an indifferent question!   meant for two?
no wonder   a story endlessly depends or fades

9
Because it couldn't be contained I suppose   I'll
quote someone quieter in the landscape   a line's
true substance not more and never less   arith-
metic makes up the necessary   number's quick
to play   with people to play time's meaningless
though a cloud advises care   did you notice it?
a cautious desire out driving   matter for fact

10
I don't know about you but my attitude is ready
to threaten a look of almost calm surprise   if
I make strenuous efforts can you apply some of
that *appropriate force*?   10° below isn't entirely
out of the question   beauty always has the time
and place   nowadays acting the common rascal
finds it hard to get a look in   icicles *will* drop

11
Charity wants out   the valley's ringed with fire
but everyone's wishes are well on course   a cup
or two to stem the tide   I'm not for a moment
trying to make it an occasion though lights out
watch them can't come quick enough   really I've
had my fill of rigor and partings are not my line
of country   when giving's hard to get I'm gone

12
When she sets out to demonstrate the fact she's
losing sight of nothing can come between us   a
weather suspending any sense of self is right by
me   my output owes little or nothing to the
storm and isolating the flash on film's a thing of
the past   it represents a move that's irresistible
I'm loaded up for the excursion she's my guide

13
For all their melancholy they're neither mutable
nor dim   as expected   the like of which I tend
to keep on ice   close up I'm laying in colour of
a near to natural hue   it's strata and scree dark
figures and sky that provide the kind of window
I've needed for years   one day I'll be happy to
have ghosts tell it   the vivid rush down nerves

14
She appreciates doesn't she the specialist folios
with accompanying gilt?   basic education in the
trance is welcome but hardly essential   I know
she keeps a good fire going   shadows by her
side for the way we turn the pages that matter
(slowly is quite enough) the history of touch is
mostly circumspect   excesses of light look bad

15
I am currently after an international product so
remote it's liable to escape the benefits of space
a second longer and I'm fixed in amber   only a
map can deliver the mind   some look on inter-
mediaries as a *byword* to more satisfactory data
nothing prepares me better for the scale of our
work!   I leave real images helpless on the plate

16
Starting out again is no option on any schedule
of mine he said   there's scope for freshness in
dis-ease but you need an eye for it   a district
free to drive the common quote or a place I've
attracted the sun   is everything either done or
pre-apocalyptic?   destiny's proofing a beautiful
friendship   as he says it's still discovering art

17
Our guide is knowing on afternoons like these
an encounter with the wind a narrative undoing
insights   he's instantly in touch with dreams of
panic!   hibiscus is his art of the present taking
its purple passages to heart   unspotted endings
aside he's changing character by rote   softly a
broken clock strikes 13   if only to sum us up

18
Somewhere gracing the radar there's talk of more
of the same   state organs and secret files   as if
you never knew the delicate transitions any move
makes   come what may you can shoot the back-
ground of a narrative head-on   you can trick the
fake out front   still networks run their stooges
reel by reel   it's near the knuckle   words divide

19
Well I've posted up my resignation!   doing the
best I can   I'm totally awake to the uncollected
life   isn't it about time someone set things out
on general offer?   (prices attached)   a case to
make surely for stealing what's laughingly called
'good cheer'   but I'm not the first to send you
to distraction   did I think you'd raise a glass?

20
The situation's proving almost too good to bear
the loss of familiar landmarks is a special thrill
when I hear your voice the elements take me at
my word and sing along   one zephyr knows me
dare I say so for an angel   try it but only in
my dreams!   the world is curiously accepting
just enough   if not my port of call there's you

21
Geodes and pumice stone gravels from the Rhine
all break up for reference   taking a day or two
to settle back where holidays shone   like all of
us the light in distant calculations is prone to go
off course … with some encouragement crack a
brand new mystery   atypical it may be but only
for the best: an avenue of limes undoes a dream

22
As a Winter flowers as memory investigates the
mind so work collaborates on equal terms   does
genius ignore the chance and signal *wait?*   so
we'll not   we'll labour the intensive till sunset
lets us down   'be right' we hear 'be with you
soon as'   but we're shiny very very sharp   a
cold blade out for wonder   and petals of blood

23
All I interrelate all I separate and colour they're
plain enough till the *flash*   If I can't believe it
neither can I make amends or let you off the
hook   at least it's wholesome common ground
we share   not yet should we have a good time
lethal   it's a canny microscope for the future
or how it's wanted   miniature days à la mode

24
In certain places in his childhood people under-
stood all he had to say   ancestor worship was
a quality night on the town and no holds barred
be they black on black   forget the more danger-
ous haunts   he'd find his way into any mind
'things learned' made ready to fly   he'd love it
that their shady prayers had multiplied his sum!

25
A truly exciting time for partnerships   as a new world ruffles a stripey curtain with a certain lime and faintly orange 'ayre'   which is pushing it or maybe you're also on the other side attempting a reconstruction?   my sources tell me I'm far too vulnerable to colour   but I've watched so many seasons go without   your window's closing too?

26
Patchwork the effect but the word I'm hearing's linear   do you ever believe me?   occasionally there's an extra ingredient: a much much darker flavour   be it in the bloodstream or a limited visual field   wherever I find you and your neat insinuations   too loveable?   only the simplest things we work on come to something in words

27
Where are we   then a common question made for the mystery   a focus as he put it all over the shop   leaving as suddenly as it came   a tilt at intimacy and textual calm   years on the shelves acquire a fuller spectrum   yesterday? it handles him with care   Autumn's a moment getting real ... he's a long time leafing through

28
Opportunity is building for the new relationship
our car park's mostly dark as I shred the minor
documents   happily suppliers are focusing on
ivy and golden lichen for less than instant decor-
ation   rapid responses are hardly called for by
and large   work flat out and we'll stop ideas
from being stolen   I'll get my best work done

29
It's all about taking most of them with you but
a lot can happen in 90 mins   I've noticed brand
names dazzle a ghost   be quick about it   folk
I've played against are quick to cement relations
photorealism?   it's a decidedly risky kind of
move if the party's out   lights there exploring
commercial significance   look who's up for sale

30
Spirit   it's cashing the worst in: a commitment
to ideas   some see it colonising futures   I'm
willing to see my best idea of *the real* inverted
looks like scarcity inspires an effort   someone
needs to countersign the act   should I cross an
other ocean?   the blue day advertised has only
presence in plenty   as they overpaint My Life

31
Distantly there's a future that may be over but
the past that keeps us dancing occasions quite
a different outcome   collateral damage is down
to fine art and the city centre's almost innocent
of crime   old photographs leave débris flawless
as a matter of tact   in practice being nowhere
in the vicinity's no excuse   be various to time

32
Sorting through the figures she comes to natural
and unnatural conclusions   ecstasy is as vivid as
it gets   but four or five paragraphs later she's
telling me where I've been and how to safeguard
'secrets'   discovering things that don't concern's
always been her forte!   more wicked still is a
tendency to watch   each QED is naked as truth

33
If it weren't for sensitivity I'd've been in touch
if anything it's time to re-introduce emotion as
if we mean it   but the point of documentation
is to pass the buck   so shall I celebrate a full-
blown world and hoard the pages or catch the
next plane out?   tomorrow is never here when
I need it!   my answers resort to leading lights

34
Identifiable only by its cover the book witnessed
more attempts at anonymity than anyone even he
could imagine   who else could possibly be held
to account?   saints in their everlasting patience
wept to think of what in a kinder world *might* be
a study for calm or a reductionist portrait   an
I as a portable wisdom   distance carrying it off

35
Parterres and sundials   do you like the sound
of it?   painstaking Summer days blue moments
and the poem altogether easy with its lot   I'm
happy if victims choose to act it out and meet
me where their endings think me   do you see
the mazy flight of butterflies   a bumbling here
if I'm lucky   when just a white flower blooms

36
Brand leader or companion in arms?   out in the
square he did everything he was told   hard as it
was he remembered carrying favours   to safety
to the last affray as his lady smiled   but streets
were deserted and his dissertation left much to
desire   how unrehearsed it was yet how sweetly
bought   her colours captured a likeness to like

37
Just how it was he thought   through a number
of quick-fire judgments to times of unrecognised
plenty   it was fitting whatever he'd done   and
inevitable?   light instant at the switch   with
blue skies then now grey he'd made it necessary:
the break   he wouldn't touch the shelf he'd set
things on   crammed with value maybe too high

38
Fair enough the portraits had exposed the present
equally they owned up to a colourful recognition
of the past   torn by a need to turn things round
false starts and shifting shapes were like a blur
on the horizon   with metaphor for a canvas she
could slash at will   later examination found how
many accomplices there were how literal the need

39
Inspirational on a level they'll never understand
a paradox combined with dreams of angels flying
in aid   the survey team were out there on their
own with torches and a single theodolite checking
on facts   a month before the unholy storm blew
in did they 'enjoy' their practice?   or was the
word unproductive   its gamble egging them on?

40

Miracles were wiped out   distress made a meal
of it by the acre   mud huts to skyscrapers all
abandoned the zeitgeist in a rush to buy   I got
the usual feeling about clouds and linings   if
marginally underplayed   but the question itself
survived no doubt at all   a trauma coming to
fruition in a shrine to healthcare deals less tax

41

Who's actually signalling intent?   who's ready
to celebrate a loophole or manage systems?   I
watched the small boats leaving harbour   blue
or red as I elected putting the economy first
is there really anything wrong with the nets we
fall through?   I'd handline a minister's long-
term reputation if I had the nous   excuses fit

42

We're taking the politics out of entertainment?
same faces painting up the town   I've seen to
the stairway heaven knows   and still safe ditto
the lift?   well everyone *I* know is happy   but
no-one's looking voters in the eye at least not
yet   like taking a night away from our dirty
dancing   add goodtimes on for good behaviour

43
Little and often?   hardly respectable returns on
the time laid out   perhaps the best of crimes
started with a yawn   after coming up with such
a story dreaming took a bit of a dive   but that
was where the likeness ended   the day itself saw
character realigned   snow lit the stranger for a
scene where words shone white enough to steal

44
Put me down for the next new conversation if
you will   according to the met we're in for a
week of Sundays and it's getting to the point
where shadow's running out   you really mind?
it's true it's all I had to hand   if only late
night scheming'd kept us up—nothing's ever
is it guaranteed   sealed units're a pain to fix

45
Was it the best the high tide had to offer?   I
ordered quite a different fit but the word's only
so reliable   someone calling out her name and
trading in turquoise might have saved the day
as it was the present dwindled and I found my-
self entitled only to texts to come   let her fix
the line of beauty   give jetsam back its wave!

46
There's a legend up there somewhere   night is
fixing an altogether imaginary point ...   draw
breath again   'it's the one we're waiting for'
is how he puts it   somewhere out of Cygnus
streams of particles of light and colour prime
his canvas   a low-level indulgence   and is he
feeling closer lovesick   abstracted to the self?

47
Surfaces to dwell on   a biography to repair the
old 'what if' ...   landscapes offer a much too
negative space   I'm embarrassed by a field on
fire   when signposts lead me nowhere do I trial
a bolder illusion?   as incidents go it's hardly
memorable!   a catalogue hugely sympathetic
accompanies the exhibition   not a window fills

48
The more restrained it is the more she mimes
till everything natural even the plainest kind of
beauty looks overprinted   even scarily blurred
more evidence of fiction and how it clouds her
sky   which is how she likes it intimate with
desperation   time to get back to base   her
outlines fading ...   acts of suspicion and faith

3.
Theatre

Planned Response

Insubstantial ...   but then it's a gift of twilight
neither one thing nor the very last word   being
in it together's cause for long-term speculation
the minuteman ready even now to plot a course

So count me down as I tell half-hidden spinneys
how he painted them   all shadow and unbelievable
yellow   one world with a ghost of a chance   so
belief shines through   by twelve if a clerk can't

Make it it's all downhill   or a day to remember?
on tricky ground   no rest but forgive me this
my trespass   seeing the paint lie good and thick
and only yesterday   still coming to terms with

The word as he saw it   mind *and* matter   with
dark the balance (the gallery too white to go by)
it's time to work his trail   to interact with any
and every finding   (history?   even yesterday's

Is saying the same ...)   let gravity track me in

Involvement

Would I like to think it matters?   the longing
for shade and a change of style   that anything
affording presence might wipe the detail   or
a grassblade rid of all private focus make for

The better companion   seldom on such a scale
but then the morning takes an opposite direction
hospitable and wild   a passing place for natural
justice   traffic like you've never seen it headed

For the single track   if the sun is out of sight
there's a glow of half-substantial evidence over
dew   I am not for painting a wood by numbers
but when a boundary presses I'm happy to take

A guide   it's the manner determines the subject
the last time things went literal I found myself
unfit to evoke   repainting touching up   even
cancelling a date   it's all there in the notebook

New propositions colour up quite nicely   as
sleet falls so my concentration takes in less and
less of the mere particular   I'm sold on making
sense of punctuation   assistants to catalogue

All the broken forms and light a moment dims

Conservation

Not that it happened overnight   an installation
gravid with a wonder all its own   did I guess
the origin of those delicate and mute obsessions
or care how the armatures extended?   keeping

Clear provided a finer judgement   long languid
lines and aborted endings dashed with red might
do for an afterthought   but this was much too
generous   I'd seen too much already as petty

Or even narcissistic   lending memory a curious
eye   leave history out of it   I'll take the first
facsimile   anything more is less   as light spills
automatically up and down the page   a vase of

Colourful occasions and some hand to rearrange
discomfort   not much to ask of habit   hardly
recognised by the crowd   at the risk of closing
ranks I ask for a pause   for interpreters used

To fiction and origin   nothing now approaches
midnight more nervously than the public dream
with the best of reasons shockproof   if proof
is needed the period 1930–1940 packs it in   to

Better appreciate its scope check out the least
responsible angle   it's always nice to find your
self?   like nobody she's ever likely to know in
the picture   mechanical and/or mystical devices

The recent work is just as fetching in the raw

The Preconditions

Beyond the summerhouse and the derelict future
they could read off one exotic interval after
another   I could see you waiting and the word
too full for a quick decision   last connections

Ready when the distances closed   cold politics
a place in the sun   but what if the diary lied?
I was out to alternatives revisiting the saved ...
don't second-guess me   a smoking ruin builds

The better house   imagination works the night-
store just as hard as you want   if you're feeling
exposed get back to basics   I can't say fortune
has me by the throat   love's cheaper and makes

For more open country   don't they care to join
us?   the shaded deckchair the blue-black cordial
eying up of books by the left   it's hard to read
them   not for want of capital   so I'm trashing

Any unwanted function   given the chance   it's
what today careers regard as the safer form of
'transport'   an elevated path or real community
service?   essential costs relate to one thing and

Often but not reliably another   futures are only
a matter of part-time grey   lots more to it of
course than that   shall we take a stretch down
by the lake maybe hear a songbird?   nightfall's

All about mild expectation   the Edwardian key

Tokens of Plenty

Spent much of the day imagining nature   when
illustration decided to rest its case   persistence
is something you tend to take for granted but
whether there's meaning in the air   or whether

The colour is all one-sided no-one will say   I
fall too readily for the labours of Spring   in
that I'm not the first and exhilaration makes for
first-class entertainment   don't look too closely

All loneliness is out of the palette   the brush
attracts whatever's confused   for contaminants
the crooked and the unashamed   it's every poor
boy's dream when a composition starts to bite

Last night the crows were on a mission   every
garden gave rise to handsome music   as if the
guilty at last faced trial   but government?   it
has left us blindness under wraps an elusive life

Should we reveal ourselves?   (a violent moment
laying on sienna)   experience the gallery window
letting us out   who's getting any younger I ask
for confirmation   who's taking on silence now

The divided self is breathtaking in its admittedly
precarious landscape   it's all routine a game for
the easily persuaded   I'm tired of insomnia   a
day that's non-essential   who's wanting fashion

Cawing from the treetop?   decorate this space

Disappearances

Pestered on and off through the night by patches
of moonlight and changes of angle   it's not the
first time a still life has got the better   there is
much more serious industry under a cloud   for

The life of me   presenting tokens cracks no ice
nor does a waking dream when dark things out
of nowhere get in first!   conspiracies?   I can't
say I've given them a chance   still my daytime

Has a way of engineering thought   which come
a certain mix of habits can set me up   have you
seen it yet?   the yellow half-light or that silver
stream?   all conscious matter is a man's delight

And terror   my place is getting like a beggar's
palace!   that or a hovel   it depends which way
you look   pictorial convenience has always been
the quick way out and I'm starting to think it's

Time to go   the limes outside my frame (could
it be too long ago?) are shaking   the old place
scatters leaves   as Summer hits new levels I
swear I'll reject all bogus offers   an honest fix

Is worth any number of wasted hours   let's see
what the mirror says or the untried brush   if
nothing else I can search the attic for some new
disorder   idealism reads obituaries like a crash

Of thunder   so who is it out there under trees?

Silvertown

It was foolish but it was history and I'm happy
you wrote it   a red crane and a camera filming
nothing of consequence   just leaving a space for
straightness in the air as we imagined it   loving

Doubt and guaranteed exile   oh shrill enough for
the word you felt for   wasn't it mother out of
sorts when the long procession passed   all flags
and sandwiches bugle and drum   now each of us

Trialling miracles   it's not impossible   by this
time tomorrow fires will scar the hillside   only
small-scale development counts itself in quids?
so far and so very natural   to sleep with justice

In arrears   but this was her voice brother and
didn't we know it   when the glass came in and
emergency saw there was time to go   a place
out west   or what   speedreading off the walls

Theatre

When and only when such dialogue treats me to
an unimpeded sunset will I fix my seal   do I
hear a little crescendo building?   somewhere
between the definite article and more abstraction

The lift is going nowhere obviously   her studio
is just another mute occasion   doesn't anyone
care?   a sentinel can't watch forever   she's all
for minimising trade   a long word in a scarlet

Envelope works fine   it must be the crackle of
history woke us to its voice   but is it likely an
actor played the part?   rehearsing distance and
even unheard conversation offers 'inspiration'

A thin acrylic stain spreads out and over every
half-won composition   madder could well be the
colour of choice   as if one gesture catches it!
silly to measure the words in paint but there's

Always an innocent temptation   she can exit if
she wants   the lights are up   and 'indifference'
can't raise its game   slow down   reframe the
unasked question   exultation hardly carries let

Alone translates ... the sitter this morning's half
in shadow half removed   too much to scrape
away?   could it be a series will suit her better?
the wildflower she is trying for takes up neutral

Ground   a running sentence   continuous desire

Collected Times

Winter after Winter ... a spell of likely weather
but never the snow that mattered   exhibits now
remind me how pavilions shone   how wine was
served blood-warm on terraces   introductions

Looking to take advantage of an excited hour
the gallery *not* inspired?   I don't believe those
rooms saw negative light   a triumph of course
but things are relative   I've a small reminder of

That time   the site itself in miniature curated
from above by red-faced men with strings   even
a chance to breathe in goodnight air   authentic
chaos   chosen as a counterweight to too much

Unintended symmetry?   all performances in art
seemed lovingly achieved   not without a certain
wit   the stars (and some you would recognise)
are on permanent standby   texts as never since

Weighed down impressively with white   it's the
anniversary murmur   nothing if not a gift to
sanity but is it true such weather freaks design?
tomorrow sees to it   every last flake's stowed

Away   so don't wait up   let the distance in

Embellishments

I listen to the darkness   cafés with blinds down
over conversations in the mind   I know too many
streets round here but not their names   will the
path appear from nowhere?   apparitions tend to

Memory in an entirely unknown weather?   it's
the interview with once loved backgrounds finds
the common chord   with textures of coldness
setting small talk off   if I know a forgery when

I see it it's down to a previous biography   all
it takes to enter another's dream world is some
self-forgetting and the will to survive   don't
stare at paintings of annunciation   its windows

Open up a vivid geometry   no chance whatever
you'll find your way   one night indeed too many
as individuals call in with the answer   disquiet
connects me   with three colours black   and a

White no images in-between   my coffee not my
trail (try anything refreshing   but words) goes
cold as again an unremembered snow begins to
settle   do I know of symphonies conducted out?

By the Wayside

Or lost in transformation? (it sometimes takes
forever) I've only myself to blame   excuse me
reality but the distance never changes   what is
said is spoken for and a glance is just a glance

Quick   as you like it (and like it you are) life
uses up the better part of its ritual   it's not
a place converts too easily into words   did we
come here often?   enough to manufacture this

Kind of trademark tear   ashamed am I I kept
amnesia under the counter?   dashing any hope
of a sale   who knows?   long curving borders
teem with colours if not new to science at least

A shock to the system   maybe the figures will
change (it's what they do) then I'll let this plot
go haywire   the book is bound   is there more
to detain you?   with inventions to your name

Already   which is why I'm dedicating midnight
to footsteps louder than the last   my A–Z's
grown as grubby as before!   what makes this
enterprise enthralling is the way a lost horizon

Never mind the time lapse sizes me up   when
harvest's over believe me you'll know the worst
re. everything I do: it's bound to realise itself
in shadow form   pick the best blooms yet or

Wait till nights draw in   we'll know the score

Indulgence

A reduction almost too easy   and so airy you'd
imagine this couldn't be got away with   really?
I'll read myself to sleep   with investigations of
a most handsome country   embedded anecdotes

Like spice then myths of a more contemporary
nature   whether cottages are lonely under the
stars hardly features in the syntax   the form's
considered   the near-on pure geometry is hard

To quarrel with   though characters sometimes
can't let go their defects can   I've seen perhaps
the best of them eyes fixed staring up at the sky
even now there's a small hiatus in the sequence

Keeping fantasy happy   haystacks read like the
midnight invitation!   a yellow moon   and the
sudden need to enter narrative   absolutely no
persuading either   procedures clearly have no

Rights where a text's concerned   if to trespass
is really meaning what it says I'm sorry   soon
as the cock crows day   (and who is it sees it
coming?) (who's ready now to let the word in?)

Is at an end   fields harvested fires out of mind

In Qualification

It's good to pursue an occasion   go far enough
back and you become its cause   am I attracting
chance?   a bird calls in the forest   the customs
man who's happy adding yet more colour to this

His schedule thinks how curious the fashion how
a secondary garden grows and whether happiness
is taken by one specific night of choice?   feels
here inside (believe me I've experienced it often)

Like someone else shaking the tree   shapes quick
to leave their mark   but I'm not getting serious
when I say the place has limits all its own   you
either recognise the change or let it pass you by

Imagine a breeze   then a purpose streaked in red
refusal?   it paints tradition   but acceptance has
better things on its mind than me   I try to
satisfy materials while back in the city it's Henri

Shifting a daydream all too willing to play   here
what's giving me double vision is the decision to
put it down   depending on how you look at it
to experience   a bird or so it seems takes wings

Illusionment

To most of those present at the time the signal
was as good as read   opened eyes or a collapse
of accepted wisdom left us nothing but freezing
rain   six months on and upstream it's far from

Navigable   but if I keep up this endless pacing
around nothing will prepare the way   can't you
have a word with tradition?   I'm arguably just
a critic of the moment and whatever the fashion

Proximity as I see it looks askance   if I sense
a colourful distinction (often a pure distraction)
in what's otherwise a poorly occupied book of
words I'll take a short cut   even to the point

Of according it the right of way   as painterly
as a concrete thought gets there's an answer to
address with questions   an innocent eye tricks
in the wording and a move to abstract distance

Treat the medium to amazing dazzle   till unlike
works with like   to a degree that puts a check
on 'limitation'   (episodes that can dam a stream
of dots and dashes)   frequency's the bonus and

Everyone's involved   be ready to respond then
if you're in the frame!   I'm out and seeing to
structures with entirely other light   a mass
of contradictory matter?   real space leaves me

A crossroads white with frost   no clearer wake

For a Simpler Song

It's easier to believe in paradise when you know
it's temporary   and understanding's mutual any
time a word gives way   I'm sinking into odder
states by the minute   or is it nothing visible's

Unique?   the boundaries once obvious seem to
favour a regular rendezvous with chance   young
people surely have proof to spare   outside my
contract or beyond this curious Summer real

Imagination mourns its loss   one side of a long
sad face the crowd is gathering for yet another
rowdy celebration   the laws are still immutable?
on evenings like this I seldom count the hours

But hold my breath and swear an oath to friends
and rank exhaustion   faint knocking in the heart
may indicate an incoming melody she says   how
generous I've been   what a dream it is   wrists

Bound perfectly with flowers   and a story too
unresearched to write!   more distance reassures
as much as dream prevails   quit now or let the
two works fuse   the world's for colouring in

In truth a street that's dark and warm buoys up

To the Sum of

It's one of those mornings   an early post and
even the plumbing starting to speak   conclusions
still unrequired?   which is why this language of
massive intent still baffles   I'm living a life as

Near to the edge as a man can fly!   it's a fold
of paper and it's always enough to be getting on
with   excitement at rubbing shoulders with the
ghost!   if 'keep clear of the mind' means what

I think …   I'm trying to put a stop to it when
a genuine hero surfaces   would I consider filling
another shelf   with bird song   with a flickering
of wings?   I reckon if only I work at it I can

Sleep forever   but dreams have a way of butting
in and I've still not taken the bait   reminding
me (also you) that a finer translation's not to be
had   till now who's monitored the closer call?

Time's come to open up or turn a tap   or else

Obscure Judgement

'I can't believe how far I've come since nightfall'
she said   'meaning's not averse to prose is it?'
flowers emerge and volumes in even the lightest
garb have aims to spare   indeed it *is* a climate

So conducive thinking's better not done   or else
I'd recommend the creamery!   top creamy ices
the old-fashioned kind with a line from Kafka if
menacing then nicely to its point   since nightfall

A couple of patrols full combat gear have scoured
the front   she speaks of perspective reflectively
as if it's known   more darkly I'd project an eye-
ful of images held in amber   and if you hold me

Up you'll be happy to see how we got here   fast
as prayer invades the understanding   'so there's
a light for all' she avers and takes the backstairs
two at a time   mute couplets?   will I ever hear

Them and never hear (I can't believe I'm saying
this) the last?   since clearly this was a wargame
with time to spare and a credible sleight of hand?
who cares   if outcomes get decided on a whim!

Stet

Subject me to a various portrait   interpret any
reflection in the mirror   present a spirit under
a suitable cloud … why not?   what used to be
just a figure in a landscape is now a medium for

Chance   additional structures are at the psychic
level   if you fix impressions you end up with a
complex fake   in confidence (?) my torments are
usually described as common   concealing reality

Delights in filling a greater whole   don't take my
word for it   the faintest shadow's a fact or it's
an argument beyond   I always preferred a good
leap over a lazy dog   not that circumstances ever

Quite abandoned 'the view'   well framed or not
I felt the need repeatedly to get out into bright
interstices   where coordinates were safe from
chance discovery or forced to run   escapements

Make for perfect small hours' reading   I have
it in myself to catch the hour   look here at out-
lines proven to square with light   (I'm not yet
on my knees)   four walls pressing for a simple

Answer think my last flower's given up a ghost

Daytime Gossip

Ultraviolet   if it's a light needs thinking about
if the occasion's right to speak I'm ticking over
and no it doesn't get harder   concern at how
everything trembles fills the darkroom   prints

Put a stop to quintessential phobias?   often he
believes   they've the kind of a mind to let a
camera be   but I'm letting no-one down as yet
so it's rumoured   just a colon leading nowhere

Is what excites   more mobile works collecting
a true life's fiction   not that anything is whole
which is why I'll catch me a glimpse on a good
day (guilt by association) and given a good time

Several really I ought no doubt to die for and
don't   disguise makes everything happen maybe
not   there's too much light to get at   all of it
for bounty and a billion years in the making so

Time enough   start loading all the impermanent
outstanding gossip   the sort that's curious
to a fault infilling spaces (unseen till much too
late) which picture stalls and traps the moment

Sees   whatever it is *here lies* and not the next

Semiconductors Etc

Can we make our minds up   can I leave it at
that   or correspond with meaning and have it
out?   close down reopen in another name so
nothing's lost   not energy not exits you can

Act on   the greatest invention tears no world
apart in the scheme of things just adds another
line   collect collect and return   know a fact
that's mobile is playing well   the usual unruly

Game   did I say unruly!   provided there's a
text outstanding there's a place love goes that
given but a breath of wind speaks well of the
short-term dead!   resources are waiting even

Now unsampled on the line   or terminal   it's
said but depends indeed on which way a good
ship's pointing   *now* you can interrupt if you
want   the magic is proof   I'm owning up to

Offhand interventions   not the first or last of
them by 'me'   insist on nothing less or your
free time back   when wires are singing I'll
reckon to hear you and the contingencies best

Interlocking Planes
after Anthony Caro

Early it is one morning   given the right   and
the right conditions   (but whom do you ask?)
you take a fair trip round yourself   consider
redefinition every bit of the way   looking hard

For the centre   and finding not what they said
you'd find   next to nothing to having it said
(and you can put this down on paper) it might
be the best work yet (there's promise for you!)

But anyway ... everyone knows   it takes more
sometimes the nocturnal regression a radiant as
well as reflected light   to be even half in touch
with it   is identity ever at home when needed?

But I do like it finished in red and welded and
bolted   it suits such a permanent construction
what happens to no-one well it happens to me!
says one line   focus shifts a whole life whole-

Sale into a state of high attention as dewdrops
ravaging a new page quit it   no there's never
the likelihood of a face   the story's yours   it
reads   convincing enough while it fills me in

Ditto Again

Knowing how to is arguably a fine art   Saturday
night was louder and less public than I thought
no-one had a chance of convincing the jury   I'm
giving nothing away when I tell you premonition

Showed up minus its habit   no statute ever read
its own obituary!   things happening out of body
either that or the occasion proved too much and
left us all bereft   keep death off the front line

Or disconnect the powerline   conscience by the
look of it dictates   isn't that what they'd say?
while back in the gallery visitors were tidying up
their words   *is emptiness a necessary retreat?*

For me all testing of the limits of art is a minor
accounting   neon and sodium and umpteen lasers
were really up to no good   if carefully disposed
but dancing in the dark?   how easy to decreate

One world or another!   refinement didn't get a
look in but memory's still preoccupied with what
seemed nothing more than a large scale rectangle
pure yellow   yellow as the word out looking for

Something   so much like itself it can't be found

Edition (Unnumbered)

To prefer one form of listlessness to another is
beside the point   we all have an axe to grind
and vehicles of persuasion these days probably
carry far fewer passengers   your call or mine?

Don't indicators warrant a brighter light?   I'll
watch performances without a thought   sorry
sights for sure when a door caves in   if only
memories of childhood turned a key   but word

Has it openings were thwarted and advances by
a highly coloured army came to nought   I see
it can be unwise to take precautions afterwards
better in fact to go down unlit roads with just

A map for company   today I'm independent of
the news   content I think to take my readings
from a changing sky   to retire is (unnaturally?)
a part of life some say   and a line of slate-blue

Cloud heading this way isn't the easiest thing
to read   safe to assume confusion and its next
door neighbour are not alone but I'm a regular
contributor to the stars   my column inches by

And large are as close as dream gets to desire

To an Ideal Space

Touchstone or millstone   open to interpretation
and visitors by appointment   foolishness is a
man who claims nothing but ignorance in matters
he's a fool to   time and again the wrong road

Gets you back on track!   and despite an April
of colossal winds I am raising A-frames like the
best   refreshment?   comes in songs the builder
himself's rephrased!   blue murder's here to be

Relied on   and sleeplessness after coming face
to face with the novel is entirely proper   I've
turned repeatedly to psalms to sing you into or
beyond the question   can't the road be cleared?

Goodwill can see how the year itself gets going
retaining a foothold down the years   if I decide
to scatter flowers in unexpected places expect me
to do it   remember natural science given half a

Chance makes a world of difference   a part in
the greater whole has nightmare where it wants
it   tonight a huge red moon is scheduled to roll
think twice if you're not for understanding   in

Any portrait there are complex articles of intent

Under Instruction

One side of the square was not so much unsettled
as trading in forgotten assets   I think I can say
I found myself at home on hearing the vendor's
call and canny response   family traits don't come

Into it or very easily not when quality's at stake
crossing over though can be quite a problem vis-
à-vis the traffic   but if velitation's not a part of
your make-up then best you stay behind   much

As I'd like to I'm still (there goes another hour)
being carried on a wave   such oily shores such
indexes of novel cargo!   I'm counting midnight's
endless blacks & blues as if a life depended on it

'Enough is plenty'   whatever the score it's good
to pass it on—no point keeping it in the family
I prefer to view the broader and hopefully longer
scene   there's something about a square   I half-

Remember   its geometry of lost occasions?   or
how it is I contain the best of the worst?   if the
work is done I lose one side of the argument and
if you make it over too just imagine the outlook!

Tactical?   realignment is the 'artifice of the day'

Herm

Mobile and interactive   it is a complete tonic to
be out and about the island   you can count the
people if there's time on your hands   yesterday
I was feeling pretty much like any horizon   one

Rainbow was bound to feel too much and anyway
trembling was permanent in the system   I had
a couple of moments when values were better left
unscrutinised and reality got the upper hand   to

Write the usual invitations seemed definitely a job
too many and in any case the crowd had other
things on their mind   material backup must be a
feature of any exploration   when I catch myself

Arranging the old familiar deal I have to strap on
a backpack and cut out all that local interference!
which of course is only half of it   the rest's in
a world of its own   in something like remission

Walking on flowers is a theatrical gift to ghosts

Cataracts

I heard it twice today   and translation wasn't in
the reckoning   home entertainment has a long
and colourful history but noir is not the drama
I've been looking for   it's never going to rhyme

With sky   if books are what you throw at the
usual busybodies the self-important geographers
of scale then maybe ascenders are right and as
maps go well off-message   why wouldn't you

Take these pictures apart?   lifting colour is a
seasonal occupation   it's a joy to experts when
perception's back in vogue   either you clear the
system under guidance   or you can watch your

Best chance crash   connectives?   even my last
is failing   what seemed initially a basis for the
good time ends its tale in shadows!   all listenable voices those I prefer are keen on acting up

And bright?   this brass clock's talking to itself

Resistance Prayer

It was both a common rule and a sombre legend
I was on my own inventing statements   how the
current in just this area of the lake made steering
almost impossible   only with the greatest effort

Did those sorrowful events maintain their almost
casual connectedness   what remained of truth
(I excuse all passing resemblance) demanded an
immense outlay of capital   did you believe in it?

In meaning stripped to light?   a shimmer is not
confined to distant waters   experience teaches us
how in countless schools of enquiry 'the new'
exists in constant fear   I am greatly impressed

If only too willing to admit to the ancient law of
'maximum price'   confessions as fraught as this
are mercury to the mind   a corrosive sublimate
or a hand to guide   not one writer can be found

Who won't confirm its 'strange affinities'   how
it will scurry into the darkest corners of hearsay
and people distance with cries of relief   how
it attaches something inviting to a life   a perfect

State?   I caution only the wisest in their station

Direction Finder

Much refreshed and unexpectedly at ease   again
this traveller was shown the way   for wasn't it
wisdom   a 'place in the desert'?   at its height
the colossus hardly short of a constructive word

It offered Strabo useful though initially private
intelligence   (who organised sales of instruments
of war   who gave the world its 'second sun')
anyway talent is what it took   300 of the same

Kind of necessary remembrance?   setting us up
in lights   as shrewdly as to allow a nice return
on capital   levying duties also a sacrificial space
in the canon   don't please mistake this beam for

Reason   (beacons growing zealously in number)
it can furnish an entrance to any intending craft
and log the data (as of old)   the very simplicity
adds to stature   it's true there's much to steal

Dry seasons always the best and steady doubting
which the best way in   if yesterday was barren
today is coming into its own   I begin to see
the 'elements of all things'   how outlines prepare

To write foundations as futures bright to receive

Future Archive

Eight indications of complicity and I can't think
since I counted them of one!   however much I
terrorise the happening it still won't come apart?
tomorrow there'll be a festive recitation   guilt

With fractals and light in nature's own pavilions
nothing remains of course of the historic sky or
underworld but do expect collective 'reinvention'
there's dream on the prowl and the whiff of joy

Seeing that syntax has found itself a glade to be
glad in I'm joining others in a choicer kind of
abandon   there's even a place for reconditioned
matter provided the horizon quoted's overseen—

In vision *and* out of this world?   it's a contract
all about changes in the weather   and in which
we're playing for all we're worth   but no there
isn't the time to question an ice floe   or add

To temperature   I suggest the party stay put
and carry on talking   make the most of popular
decisions the gaudy majorettes indeed the local
aqua-vitae till it's safe to turn our backs   is it

That mystery item 9?   who cares what's next!

Bounteous Shore

Well could it be?   I knowingly wasn't the first
there was too much going to wrack and ruin no
castles to build   and pirates away to respectable
locations east of eden left me no maps ... I *will*

Follow but for just this once please steer   torn
papers torn silk   the rigging's some other kind
of business and the quality of all this expectation
can't be bought   I'll save you whatever there is

I can where can't is a useful option   be sure to
see to things if lights start challenging the sky
get over the water to a calmer truth   plainness
of driftwood or feint of the mind   a solo chant

My drift is hard on the eye its darkness comes
a-calling   only a log of impossible intimation
don't count on silver ...   my settings all show
up exactly as they will   or leave this moment

To another past for rescue   now I'm sailing in

Hankering

So if it isn't an hour for solace maybe it's two
before it happens   I have all day and half-time
inclinations to rely on   semi-precious indications
meaning   a word for taking is the word to use

In holding such questions maybe it's carrying
business to extremes   when nature's just on the
outside images go haywire and our curtains fall
no it's not an innocent squall   I'm blacking out

The scene for safety   appearances are anything
anything's better in a stopped machine   you
know I've been here till my eyes are red   'who
is it and who installed the meter'   one meeting

Never makes it to the news or pulls the crowds
in—I've seen better openings at a fête   when
you're trialling madness nothing is better surely
than the kiss of death   to be seen to wait here

Patient in the queue for answers isn't love alive?

Elaboration

Sweet chestnut keeps its distance   cool as any
morning   white convolvulus   come closer it's
tinged with pink   for getting personal tell me
about interaction   how structures branch and

Keep it from no-one getting heavy-handed with
doubt   my micro-history   my summary of
a day in history   undone by a question   as
I see through nature to who knows what   idea

The very thought of it   giving up the wary the
'approach with caution'   'proceed with care' …
it's enough to type your name in even the what
and why if anyone asks   who's been here and

Gone   tomorrow's as striking as its text   and
a twist in the stem can trap your finger (was I
to say 'on a day like this'   I was and know it
never is) and not your mind   belief's hardly a

Last-ditch entertainment just a word for flower

Monday Prologue

It is about to rain   as far as one can tell it is
business as usual   a green arch advertising
numerous products set in bright white squares
and families negotiating all that they have to

Wherever they are whatever a thought intends
it's not a special offer   nothing so ordinary as
a story cut from the bone but there's evidence
of history here   rewriting how the front-line

Characters stole a march   no-one's about to
change the date surely?   without a thought for
trailing life through dust   when music pipes its
way to the purse I'm ducking out   some plot

The movement others examine entrails my view
is see what else will change   be changed or let
time trick itself as the trucks roll in   a cabinet
of greater or lesser affairs   I strike a deal with

Innocent persuasion   and the hardest thing to
fight?   these shoppers mostly off their guard
stump up   as doors swing rapidly to a range
of heroes 'redefined'   for bloodless revolution

Small change talks   it's a mystery looking up

To Independence

I tried not to believe it but there was nothing I
could do   it was an expanse of reliable shadow
each and every excursion took me closer to the
mark   between the picture and a shift in focus

Only the one thing intervened?   as if intended
and clearly a million miles from neutral   with
experience on its side it occupied no more than
it had to—obvious emotion in its valid space

A white-out   a long awaited falcon somewhere
over the cliff and the route unknown   were I
alone there would be no indication and I would
be loathe to track it down but together there's

Potential   for rockfall or skyfall   immediacy in
its element   if I call up pieces of the melody
haphazard and as likely new it's still a shock to
the system   I didn't mean to entertain nor did

I try for special effects but interludes (on such
a day) are everything   to remember the first
time is to return forever to a place you never
knew   I'm under its leaves and safe as houses

When the moment came I took its name as real

Graphic Paradox

Almost by accident you'd think but the 'yellow
biplane' had a mind of its own   for once the
sky was cloudless and it was easy to count up
all those reasons for doubt—would he agree?

But then it was just a photograph   any place
prior to 1960 a gift   revealing as much to con-
ceal the 'tyranny of meaning'   easing back on
the throttle—whatever you like—not likely

To stall or fuss when one of the worlds played
up and spun   imagined distances   too vast to
hold?   not even once   not for the chance to
entertain an eye but rather play the nondescript

With words   forever about to crash   and life
left flying safe from questions   happy to turn
the smoke on and have a secondary wind blow
arrogance or anything like it clear   off course

No accident   the sky's been ragged ever since

Paper Transfer

Spot the error   no you can't see sky when it's
dark?   or admire the truth and catch that some-
one sneaking by   in bar-room terms it's public
spirited enough   to make you weep at the top

Of yet another News I can underline the caption
no-one'll know the price if days are written out
in small print!   futures when you reach them
'slammed'   keys lost   I'll drink to nothing less

Who else owns up   is it anyone I know or just
a dream?   maybe nothing itself lies overhead
blue heavens they're truly yours in the meantime
really I need some time to reconnoitre a distant

Field   think about scenes like this depicted on
an average card I'm right back where my past
broke out or tried to   what *is* interfering now
(supposedly?) (it's out of a 'sense of duty') is

The absent mind   thought meaning oh so well

Courtly Love

It has to be said   you're leaving nothing at all
to chance   travel through airy wastes poses no
problems when evenings of departure read like
this   again you're taking my world for granted

Every need's available   in dream and devotion
in 'rivers *lost* for early morning light'   so I
took one phrase to make it more exact—does
that make me now your fool?   seems like half-

Forgotten time   a legend to hide one face and
show another (bureaux claim no record of your
moods or moves)   having someone decorate an
empty room when the cold winds bite   a word

And persistent here   in *vespers* tracking me to
unlikely truth   if six out of seven tricks seem
impossible in context one works a treat!   else-
where the print unravels   not a ball of string

But it'll do for a start   whoever makes an end

Decline in Use

Results in loss of optimism   facilities I knew
describe a line that's totally other   plots now
if not anonymous keep sources under wraps or
deny involvement   where riot leads to history

And history riot there is never a hint of self-
expression to relate?   as profit drives ideas to
connect   where I found my feet I saw 'the
machine' itself was inspirational to a fault   far

From imitating fame it had attached its gift to
fact   so much for the decent heart and hope
spine-tingling romance might keep the best on
edge   the worst laid plan went on to would-be

Greater things as codes and small print tricked
us out   no second-guessing no 'getting into it'
for luck   it was all or nothing and like for like
one universe and everything it's what you hold

And tantamount to debt   unpaid   with bailiffs
baling out in cloud   I've gone the long way
round and kept my claim on hold whatever an
angel says   it's as well to entertain the threat?

Tomorrow's straight and narrow tempts me out

Authority

'It was firelight on another world   it was as if
a new voice sang'   but you can't go anywhere
and consciously you can't go home   at a time
life's otherwise if studiously engaged   too soon

Or it may be everything's recorded like a dream
or so they believe the text misunderstood   in-
consequential   bit by bit untouchable like light
on water tempting what?   protection please not

Causes calling up a future   the pattern's hardly
set when a word translates surprise   as change
and change are never and not for nothing quite
the same   it seems 'fruition' et al has much to

Answer for   my folk and others watching fire-
works (on a nightly basis) dialogue with what?
when I take the first train out   blinds down on
self for an unthought fractured history of love

It's natural?   or it may be soon enough   I'm
freeing up horizons with forgive me my oldest
dark excuse   soon yours as ever truly   makes
the world go round   don't list my symptoms

Tell me everything I partly knew or not or else

www.ingramcontent.com/pod-product-compliance
Lightning Source LLC
Chambersburg PA
CBHW031157160426
43193CB00008B/410